A FRESH NEW START

THIS BOOK IS
A SPECIAL GIFT

TO:

FROM:

DATE:

MESSAGE:

A FRESH NEW START

SOLLY OZROVECH

Christian Art Gifts

A FRESH NEW START by Solly Ozrovech

Originally published in Afrikaans under the title *'n Lentekans tot 'n nuwe lewe* by Christian Publishing Company.

English edition published by Christian Art Gifts
PO Box 1599, Vereeniging 1930, South Africa

First edition 2001

Designed by Christian Art Gifts

Translated by M.J. Kruger

Following the New International Version, pronouns referring to God are written in the lower case for the sake of consistency. The American spelling variants of the New International Version have been retained, but the contents of this devotional follows the British spelling system.

1-86852-777-8

Printed in Hong Kong

01 02 03 04 05 06 07 08 09 10 – 10 9 8 7 6 5 4 3 2 1

A FRESH NEW START

TABLE OF CONTENTS

ONE

—*—*—*—*—

CHRISTMAS ALL THROUGH THE YEAR

Lettie Roos, the woman who raised me, was an expert canner of peaches. They were called Cala peaches because they were originally grown in Cala in the Transkei. Around Christmas-time we tucked into these delicious peaches with fervour, and at the same time Aunt Lettie was canning away!

She was an artist at it: boiling the syrup according to her own secret recipe; sterilising the bottles with steam; knowing which rubber rings were best for sealing the bottles; peeling and cutting up and stoning the fruit. The final products were masterpieces inviting you to feast on them.

However, the canned fruit was destined for the pantry shelf where the bottles stood regimented in rows, waiting for those piercingly cold winter nights that are so well known to every "Kapaailander."

Town and farm folk loved visiting Uncle Gys and Aunt Lettie on winter nights. Late at night the expected mystical ritual was enacted when one of her bottles was taken from the pantry shelf. Even the children could share in the ensuing feast. It was an indescribably delicious extension of midsummer!

When I was a child I often wondered why people couldn't can the Christmas spirit for use during those frost-bitten and snow-covered winter nights ... Why should the Christmas spirit last only one month or even one day in a whole year?

There are some people who know the art of extending Christmas.

Last year, at around the end of March or beginning of April, we were driving through Keimoes on our way to Augrabies in the Northwest Province. In front of the municipal building in Keimoes we saw it: the whole length of the street was bordered with roses in full bloom. A sea of white blooms were alternated with red ones: a joy to behold and an inspiration to the exhausted traveller.

A feast for the heart – Christmas in April! Here was a town council telling visitors with roses how welcome they were. Suddenly I was homesick for Aunt Lettie – she loved flowers fervently.

If you have ever had the privilege of travelling between Robertson and Bonnievale in the Boland you will also know what a "canned Christmas" means.

This is vine and horse country. However, the farm women provide a wealth of flowers on both sides of the road. Climbing roses and other roses alternate with cannas in every imaginable colour, competing kilometre after kilometre in providing the traveller with joy.

These flowers do not provide any income for the farm and need a lot of labour and care. Even so, there they are, growing in abundance for the enjoyment of every passer-by: a Christmas gift in October from the diligent women of the district.

I heard about a little girl (who has her birthday in August) who received an extraordinary gift. Last year on this joyful day she ran to her parents, embraced them and called out excitedly, "Thank you Mummy, thank you Daddy! This is the most wonderful gift I have ever received!"

What was the gift causing so much joy?

A letter from two parents telling their ten-year-old daughter: "Mummy and Daddy have decided to give you, in addition to your other gifts, the gift of ourselves: every day of the week one full hour and every weekend two full hours per day – time of love!" Christmas in August!

God loved at Christmas, and he gave his Son for Christmas and for the whole year. Every time we give a part of ourselves it is Christmas in our hearts and all around us. Do I imagine hearing sounds of joy in heaven?

Once, in wintertime, I held a service in the little town of Rhodes, situated on the way to Barclay East in the ravines of the Drakensberg. It is so bitterly cold there that it is one of the few places in our country where people can ski in winter.

That morning the countryside was covered in

snow and we had to drive very carefully to the church. The motorcars were parked closely together around the church as if the building was generating some heat to combat the worst of the cold.

How correct this impression proved to be. During the singing of the first hymn I could count twelve Queen stoves glowing cosily along the walls on both sides.

The crooner, Bing Crosby, conquered the world with his song "White Christmas." These were the words flashing through my mind that day on the pulpit: a white Christmas in the middle of winter. Time upon time that morning my thoughts turned to Christmas, so that ever since that day I have always associated Rhodes with Christmas.

Just outside Robertson, on the way to McGregor, there is a lane of bluegum trees. The gigantic trunks stand far apart, but in the sky the branches intertwine over the road to form a heavenly dome above the passer-by.

On our way to friends we saw two people walking hand in hand in the shade of the trees, secure in their love and not at all shy to show it to the world.

"The woman is pregnant," Louise observed in passing.

We gave them a lift to their humble dwelling at McGregor. They were two beautiful Christmas people giving themselves to each other – every day in the year. Christmas in November.

This "Mary" didn't have a donkey to ride upon, but the "Child" was there ... in the canned Christmas spirit of people even in the November of life!

TWO

—*—*—*—*—

CAST YOUR BREAD UPON THE WATERS

Of course, right-minded people do not perform acts of mercy with a reward in mind. Nevertheless, what the writer of Ecclesiastes says is true: *Cast your bread upon the waters for after many days you will find it again* (Ecc. 11:1).

We were driving with our first-born along the long road from Pretoria to Paarl. It was swelteringly hot and the heat waves were shimmering on the tarred road. Between Beaufort West and Laingsburg our trustworthy Peugeot 404 suddenly stopped short and obstinately refused to move another metre.

I have always been a proponent of the idea that every student in theology should take a short course in motorcar mechanics: we spend quite a large percentage of our time clutching a steering wheel.

However, like many of my colleagues, I have little knowledge of the secret workings of this most comfortable of all vehicles. Up to that day our Peugeot had never, no never, had any problems. That is why his pet name was "Pure Joy."

But standing there at three o' clock that sweltering afternoon on the Karoo plains, I regretted my lack of knowledge of the workings of a motorcar.

The baby was irritated, there was no more milk in his bottle, the motorcar had broken down ... and one after another the cars passed us by as if we were part of the landscape.

Later I opened the bonnet of the engine as a kind of emergency signal. In vain. The cars continued to glide past.

Around six o' clock we were becoming really anxious and the baby was screaming. Then a Good Samaritan and his wife stopped for us and enquired whether we had problems. Undeserved grace: the man was a motorcar mechanic. I looked in undisguised admiration at this earthling who had so much useful knowledge.

After about twenty minutes the car was repaired and roadworthy. We started chatting with our benefactors, refreshed by the delicious coffee supplied by the wife of the Samaritan. They were from Worcester, the hometown of my wife, Louise.

Yes, he had known her father well; everybody in Worcester knew Uncle Dawie du Toit. He then proceeded to tell us this almost unbelievable story.

Years ago our Samaritan and his new bride had had a breakdown between Laingsburg and Worcester. At that time he was still an apprentice at a garage. Even his knowledge was not enough to get them on the road again and nobody wanted to stop.

In the end a friendly man stopped and offered help. He towed them to their house in Worcester.

The Samaritan? Dawie du Toit, father of the girl with the baby on the hip. My eyes became misty – such a coincidence occurred only once in a lifetime!

When we drove home that night we first said thank you – Up High, of course. We thanked God for the Samaritan and his wife and Father Dawie who never passed anybody in need!

Something altogether different happened to Nakkie Dykman, Louise's grandfather, at that time the principal of the school in Rawsonville. Grandpa Nakkie was a dignified and respected man who did everything painfully correctly. He was also the proud owner of one of the early Model T Fords.

They were on their way back from Cape Town. In those days a visit to Cape Town was a smart occasion. Grandpa Nakkie was wearing his best suit. Grandma Dykman was also a smart woman. She was proudly wearing her best dress, complete with hat, gloves and parasol.

About ten kilometres outside Paarl Grandpa Nakkie saw an identical Model T Ford standing at the roadside. One side of the car was jacked up and the other side was balanced on a heap of stones. Trouble with both wheels at once?

"A brother in need!" the softhearted Grandpa Nakkie voiced his thoughts. In spite of Grandma's protests Grandpa pulled off the road, planning to stop behind the vehicle in need. "It behoves a Christian to lend a helping hand," he explained to Grandma.

What went wrong was unfortunately not transmitted to posterity. In his Samaritan zeal Grandpa had forgotten to step on the brake pedal soon enough and he drove right into the back of his fellow car owner's treasure.

The little Ford was neatly pushed off its perch on the jack and the heap of stones, and collapsed completely. Consternation! A furious man in need, whose hours of work had been undone, was glaring at an embarrassed Samaritan trying to explain what had happened.

Fortunately more help arrived, calmness prevailed and in the end everybody returned home satisfied. It is said that Grandma was still pale and furious about this "irresponsible incident" when they came to the other side of Bainskloof.

Fortunately this event doesn't mar the truth of the comment made by the writer of Ecclesiastes about the bread on the water. As Grandma said later when she had calmed down, "It is the thought that counts."

Keep up your spirits, all you good people who cast your bread upon the water without thinking of profit: mothers who raise babies; fathers who teach their children to bear difficulties in a dignified manner; teachers who spend their lives guiding children towards adulthood; sports coaches who spend hours of their valuable time to produce champions ... We remind all of them of the Great Caster of bread who died on a rough wooden cross so that he could become the Bread of Life for us. May his loving deed never prove to have been in vain in our lives.

THREE

—*—*—*—*—

THE SPICE OF LOVE

Easter is the festival of the unimaginable, the seemingly impossible, the unbelievable. It is the festival celebrating the conquering of death and everything associated with it: the triumph of an empty grave and a resurrected Saviour.

In Israel where these events took place it is spring during this time of the year. I think this fact makes a significant difference to the perceptions and convictions accompanying our experience of this day.

The glorious message of the resurrection is proclaimed and confirmed in creation by new life all around: the easter lilies announce the good news on their waxen trumpets; the birds spontaneously start singing their song of praise at the break of day; every flowering tree and flaming bush is a living proclamation of the glory of the resurrection.

May this joy glow in our hearts today.

As so often in the life of the Master, women played an important role on this day. This fact may also open up some new perspectives for us. These women were attached to Jesus by means of an unbreakable bond of deep love. This is what urged them to visit the grave early that morning.

All other things were of less importance and soon forgotten. They knew the wonder of going to the Lord on wings of love early in the morning. If we do this, the day will bring forth no unmanageable evil and we can tread our way lightly.

It was the same constant love which made them walk with him, which made them stand at the foot of the cross and which made them faithful even unto the grave. Love is stronger than death.

With their hands filled with fragrant spices they proclaim to the unbelieving and hostile world that they are on the side of the despised Man of Nazareth. Their spice-filled hands tell those who want to hear: we are not ashamed of our Master.

To be the bearer of spices is a noble calling, but it is not always easy. Just ask anybody urged by love to work in some part of God's kingdom: those keeping vigil and comforting at a sickbed; those who are free with their smiles and warm handshakes; those who support a fellow human being who has fallen; those who pray in their closet for children and parents alike; those who bring the gospel to hungry heathen hearts. They exude a lovely fragrance, like these women from Jerusalem; they are spice bearers in life.

However, for these women there was a stumbling-block which could obstruct their task of love: a stone in front of the opening to the tomb. However, they did not allow themselves to be thrown off balance. With typical feminine loyalty they calmly persevered on their way – and to their joy and surprise the stone had already been removed. They did their duty without hesitation and the Almighty sent his angel to remove the stumbling-block.

"Who will roll the stone away from the entrance of the tomb?" These words touch upon the most profound mystery of life. The English author, Sir Francis Bacon, said in one of his essays that men fear death as children fear walking in the dark. Shakespeare spoke of death as "that uncharted land from which no traveller has ever returned."

No ransom can be paid to escape death, for all of us are destined to die. Who will roll this stone away for us?

Great philosophers have tried to answer this cry for help – unsuccessfully, because human hearts have remained broken. Poets and singers have written poignant and beautiful songs about it. Sculptors have represented death as a marble angel with an extinguished flare in the hand. However, to gloss over death does not mean to conquer death. In doing so the stone has not been moved a hair's breadth.

The great British author C. S. Lewis called the resurrection "the supreme miracle in which God leaned against the flywheel of history and reversed its direction." God is the only One who can give an answer to this great mystery. He let it happen before the eyes of the women at the tomb: the stone was rolled away, the entrance was open, the seal was broken, the grave was empty!

Shakespeare, you have it wrong. Somebody did return from that uncharted land. He triumphantly conquered death. Bacon, you have it wrong: yes, fear and hesitation will still be there, but he is there also to lead us through the dark valley. Death is dead ... and Christ lives!

The coat of arms of Spain originally carried the motto, "Ne plus ultra" – "there is nothing further" – meaning that Spain had already discovered the entire known world. However, Columbus discovered a whole new world in 1492. Then the motto was changed to "Plus ultra" – "there is much more."

Before Christ death was final. However, with his resurrection a new world was opened. Now the grave is merely the shining entrance-hall through which we enter into the glorious crystal-clear brightness of heaven. No eye has seen, no ear has heard, no mind has conceived what God has prepared for those who love him, his spice bearers in life.

May your faith in the glory of his resurrection roll away the stones of life for you and give you hope in the face of life as well as death.

In northern countries Christians greet each other on this day with a special greeting: "The Lord has risen!" which is answered with "The Lord has truly risen!" A blessed Easter to everybody who bears spices for him on this day.

A HAPPY
HEART MAKES
THE FACE CHEERFUL

PROVERBS 15:13

FOUR

—*—*—*—*—

ANCHORS IN A STORMY SEA

We hear of so much sorrow and pain these days. The silt-dam disaster at Merriespruit is still vivid in our memories. Retrenchments leaving families without breadwinners are common. We are forced into an acute realisation that unemployment is one of the worst things that life can do to you. The monstrous head of violence and anarchy pops up everywhere. Mineworkers are trapped in a conflagration in a mine and die gruesomely. There are many people nowadays who are unexpectedly overwhelmed by crises, and are left with nearly incurable wounds. Is there any hope in this era of disastrous events?

The biblical Job certainly knew about such wounds after his whole world had tumbled around him. The worst that can happen in life happened to him. For him it wasn't a case of hearsay, but of sorrow lived through. He could certainly speak about wounds. It was as if an earthquake had struck his life.

We first get to know Job through a testimonial given to him in the book of comfort named after him: ... *This man was blameless and upright; he feared God and shunned evil ...* (Job 1:1).

He had ten children, sheep, camels, oxen, donkeys and a large number of servants. He was a respected man because he was known for his righteousness, diligence and integrity.

Then, without warning, disaster upon disaster struck him like an avalanche. He lost his animals, his harvests, his lands, his servants ... and worst of all, every one of his ten children. His health was blighted and with it every hope that he could ever again earn a living.

Be still for a while and try to imagine yourself in his position: overwhelmed by an unexpected avalanche of disaster, adversity and sorrow. And then read what Job said about these things that God had allowed to happen in his life: *"Naked I came from my mother's womb and naked I will depart. The LORD gave and the LORD has taken away; may the name of the LORD be praised"* (Job 1:12). Is it at all possible for a mortal man to utter such words in such adverse circumstances?

A last footnote is added to this event: *In all this Job did not sin by charging God with wrongdoing* (Job 1:22). Remarkable, isn't it? Think about the realities of insolvency, pain and sorrow, sickness and ten new graves. Despite all this Job persevered in trusting God, without calling him to account and without reproach! However is this possible? Without oversimplifying the matter, I would say that Job had a few anchors keeping him safe in a stormy sea.

Job acknowledged God's loving sovereignty. If God is the Giver he may also take. In Job's own pain-filled words it is expressed thus: *"... Shall we accept good from God, and not trouble?"* (Job 2:10). He looked up to heaven and acknowledged God's sovereignty to do with his creation whatever he wanted.

Who is the fool who remarks that the Potter may not form the clay; may not break his own handiwork to bring forth something better and more beautiful; may not put it into the oven to strengthen and refine it? Job knew that God's sovereignty is tempered by his love.

His love and omniscience will let all things work for our good. This anchor gave Job wings that allowed him to soar above his personal loss and sorrow. Job relied on the expectancy of life hereafter. This expectancy was a preservative anchor in the hour of agony. He shouts for joy in the dark: *"I know that my Redeemer lives ... I myself will see him with my own eyes ... How my heart yearns within me!"* (Job 19:25-27).

In these days, while we are standing by the empty grave to commemorate the triumphant resurrection of our Master, we would do well to listen to the Old Testament faith of this man. Can we, who have the privileged knowledge of the New Testament truths, imitate him? He looked forward to the day when everything will be new again and hope will not be disappointed; when sickness, death, suffering, unrest and violence will be no more. Job could endure the disasters because he had a living hope.

Job confessed his own lack of understanding … and that is a liberating anchor. It leaves all the whys in God's loving hands: *"I know that you can do all things; no plan of yours can be thwarted … Surely I spoke of things I did not understand, things too wonderful for me to know"* (Job 42:2). For the first time Job saw himself as God saw him and then he flew with the wings of faith: *"My ears had heard of you, but now my eyes have seen you. Therefore I despise myself and repent in dust and ashes"* (Job 42:5). Through all of Job's losses he found his God. No wonder that Job started to pray for his friends and in doing so changed his circumstances.

Marga Ley, journalist at *Beeld* in Johannesburg said about the Oppermans of Merriespruit that they, after they had lost everything, tried to smile and said, "We have much to be thankful for. We are alive."

Merriespruit and muddy silt, burning mine shafts, unrest and uproar, pain and sorrow might seem far removed from you at this moment. This is what Job too thought before the hurricane struck him. When disaster strikes in *your* life, remember where Job found the strength to gather the pieces together. The strangest truth of the gospel is the message that redemption can be born of suffering.

An Oriental saying goes: "When I am forever in the sunshine, I am living in a desert." Suffering and loss can transform your life into a paradise.

FIVE

—*—*—*—*—

BLESSED ARE YOU AMONG WOMEN

When you stand next to the obelisk at the Women's Memorial in Bloemfontein, looking up into the blue South African sky, a strange respect for all the mothers of all the ages stirs in you. You suddenly appreciate the meaningfulness of setting aside one day in the year to pay special homage to mothers.

James M. Barry wrote: "This God to whom little children pray has a face resembling that of a mother." This is not necessarily good theology, but it undoubtedly does contain some practical truth. The power of motherhood means that a mother is the one person on earth who has the greatest influence on her child. Usually she is the child's first link to God.

Charles Dickens said: "It should be written somewhere that the virtues of the mother will be ascribed to the child even as the sins of the fathers." In his first years the child experiences his mother as an ever-present and all-encompassing nurturing and protecting power. She is food, love, safety and growth to the child. To receive her love means to live, to have roots, to have an address, to be safe at home.

In this truth there lies a danger for those who accept motherhood as a matter of course. One is not a "mother" only because one has children. It is just as absurd as thinking one is a famous pianist because one possesses a piano.

Temple Bailey wrote a touching parable. Freely retold it goes like this:

"A young mother put her feet on the road of life. 'Is it a long road?' she asked. 'Yes, it is tiring and you will be much older by the time you reach the end. But the end will be better than the beginning!'

"However, the young mother was happy and she thought that nothing could be better than these years. She played with her children and picked flowers for them along the way and swam with them in the clear streams of life. The sun shone down on them and the young mother said, 'Nothing will ever be better than this time!'

"Then night fell and a storm came up. The way was dark and her children were trembling with fear and cold. The mother pulled them to her and embraced them in her loving arms and the children said, 'Dear Mother, we are not afraid, because you are with us and no evil will come to us.' And the mother said, 'This is better than the splendour of the day, because tonight I have taught my children the meaning of courage.'

"Morning came and they had a steep hill before them. The children climbed and got tired. The mother was also tired, but she kept saying to the children, 'Take courage! We shall be there just now!' So the children climbed and when they reached the top, they said, 'Mother, we could never have done it without you!' When the mother went to bed that night, she looked up at the stars and said, 'This has been a better day than yesterday, because my children have learnt the meaning of effort and perseverance. Yesterday I gave them courage, but today I have given them strength.'

"The following day threatening clouds packed together in the sky – clouds of hatred, evil and war, and the children feared the dark. They groped about and stumbled. The mother told them, 'Look up! Look at the Light!' And the children lifted their eyes up to the hills and behind the clouds they saw Eternal Glory. It led them past the darkness. That night the mother said, 'This has been the best day of all, because today I have brought my children to God!'

"When the mother grew old, her children stood strong and courageous. Where the going was rough and uneven they carried her, until they went over a hill where a shining road led to a golden gateway. The gate swung open for her and the mother said, 'I have reached the end of the journey. Now I know that the end is better than the beginning, because my children can go on their way alone.'

"The children said, 'Mother, you will always be with us, even though you have gone through the gate.' They stood and looked on as she entered alone ... and the gate swung closed. And the children said, 'We cannot see her, but a mother like ours is with us always. She is more than a memory – she is a living presence!'"

Of course it is true that one should not put only one day in a year aside to honour mothers. They deserve it every day.

In spite of all the arguments against the commercialisation of Mother's Day, the critics of the day are usually those people who want to avoid the positive duties of Mother's Day. Love is not primarily the giving of expensive gifts, but the renewed and continuous giving of yourself. Mother's Day is a day that will serve to remind you to do it all through the year – even as our visit to the manger in Bethlehem reminds us of him who gave his life for us and who urges us to live our lives for him.

For this reason we pay homage to all mothers on this day. We say to you as Elizabeth said to Mary when she heard that Mary would become the mother of the greatest Man of all ages: *"Blessed are you among women ... !"* (Lk. 1:42).

SIX

—*—*—*—*—

TRUE GIVING

Somebody once said, "Bring me flowers while I am still alive, bring me the flowers then; but when I have died, take those flowers and give them to those who stay behind!"

This truth Dawie and Martha illustrated in a practical way. Their garden on their farm near Montagu had always been a paradise where friendship could flourish among the beautiful flowers, trees and lawns.

When they moved to a retirement village at Hermanus they did not allow themselves to come to a standstill mourning for the beauty that they had had to leave behind. They started decorating their new environment with vision, love and devotion.

First they beautified the immediate surroundings of their home with the loveliest assortment of roses and other flowering plants and shrubs. Then they went across the road and up against the side of the mountain behind their home. There they started an unassuming garden in the mountain soil.

However, with these two people a garden has no chance to remain unassuming. What they have brought into being and established during the last few years is an adornment and a pleasure to the eye.

Fertiliser and manure were transported from their farm near Montagu – and here their children and grandchildren became involved with this public garden. A dam with water plants and a fountain was built, an irrigation system was added and floodlights were installed to add to the beauty at night.

The garden became bigger and bigger and more and more beautiful. The flowers grew as if the angels' seed bag described by Boerneef was opened when they flew past that spot. Birds of all kinds and sizes came to drink water and to bathe. Exotic plants intermingled with beautiful indigenous ones. Everyone who takes the trouble to look for it will find his favourite in Dawie and Martha's garden.

It is as if this garden has started a new passion and rejuvenation in the lives of these two people.

In love and devotion they have spared no cost or labour to keep this garden at its most beautiful. A bench was placed on the mountainside among the flowers. Now those who want to can sit there among the wealth of flowers, staring across Walker Bay and dreaming their dreams … surrounded by beautiful flowers that can scarcely be surpassed by Namaqualand in its best flowering season.

The wonder of this garden is that it is the possession of everybody. Daily, but mainly over weekends, people drive past slowly or stop to share in the glory of the flowers for a while.

Wedding couples come to have their photographs taken there to immortalise their glorious happiness. Mourners come and sit there to feel the comfort of the Lord seeping into their hearts. There is no boundary, fence, wall or partition – it is free, like the grace of God, for everybody to enjoy.

I may imagine it, but I think this garden has had a rejuvenating effect on the personal lives of Martha and Dawie. It is as if they are physically healthier; are ever becoming younger; always have a twinkle in the eye. It is as if a paradise is opening up in their hearts, a paradise which they freely share with others. It is as if the garden revives their spirits.

Another anonymous poet wrote:

> The song of the birds for pardon; a kiss
> of the sun for mirth;
> You are nearer God's heart in a garden
> than anywhere else on earth!

The other gardeners in the retirement village are also inspired by Dawie and Martha's garden. Every time when we visit there the neighbouring gardens are more beautiful and better cared for. Their decoration of the environment has spread out: first to their children and grandchildren, then to their neighbours and friends, then to visitors and wedding couples.

Everybody passing by involuntarily drives or walks more slowly. Birds come and bathe, drink water and sing. Here the common language of a garden is spoken across all boundaries of language and colour.

Of course it costs them thousands of rands, but they never speak about it – I wonder if they ever even think about it!

They are truly "giving" people because in reality they are giving of themselves. That is the highest and purest form of giving. In the same way Somebody long ago gave his Son to make a new, better life possible for us.

People who give of themselves, are people who create beauty where there is no beauty and who share it freely with others without expecting anything in return.

SEVEN

—*—*—*—*—

A FIRE BY THE ROADSIDE

Holiday memories form part of the frame of reference of every family. They are like an extra suitcase that you joyfully carry with you on your journey through life. Often they also give rise to witticisms and expressions that are restricted to your own family. To other people they are unintelligible and even nonsensical.

In our family, when someone asks a question to which the answer is self-evident, we say, tongue in cheek, "Oh, but she doesn't have a horse!" Family members will understand immediately and perhaps show boisterous enjoyment, but strangers will think we have a screw loose.

Every family has some of these enjoyable sayings peculiar to the group. This particular saying has its origin during one of our holidays at Port St. Johns, where we have been going on vacation for more than twenty-four years. It originated one day on the way from Umtata to Port St. Johns.

In the beautiful Llengana Pass we saw a man on horseback: straight and gallant, wearing a hat with a wide brim and regularly sending up smoke puffs from his churchwarden pipe into the unpolluted Transkei air. Behind the horse his wife was walking, one child on the hip, another by the hand … and a big bundle on her head.

"This is unfair and callous," the women remarked. We stopped a little way in front of the horse and when the calm horseman courteously stopped next to us, I wanted to know why he allowed his wife to carry the heavy bundle and why he didn't let her ride on the horse.

He turned his proud neck stiffly, looked down his nose at his wife and philosophically remarked, "Oh, but she doesn't have a horse!" With that the case was closed and he rode on. After all these years we still enjoy the honest dictum of this man.

July was my trusted angling friend and we spent many nights on the rocks of the Wild Coast or at the mouth of the Umzimvubu River – a fisherman's paradise. July was a remarkable man: a fisherman without equal, a lay preacher in his village, an honest and diligent worker, a true friend and a philosopher if ever there was one.

One afternoon we covered about twelve kilometres on foot to reach an extremely popular angling spot where we planned to spend the night. We reached it at around dusk and already there were about a dozen men who had come from the nearby village with the same intentions as ours.

I balanced my fishing gear against the rocky

wall, and somewhat worriedly I asked July whether my gear was safe there. He looked through the slits of his experienced eyes, scanned the surroundings with the eyes of a connoisseur and pronounced his considered opinion: "No, Umfundisi, no danger – there are no other white people here!"

Another much colder than usual night I asked the flimsily clad July whether he wasn't cold. No, he wasn't cold, but Umfundisi was cold. "I am really not cold," I protested, "I am wearing a warm fisherman's jacket."

"That's right," July answered, "but, Umfundisi, your head is bare."

During June the days in this Wild Coast paradise can be gloriously mild, but the nights sometimes become bitingly cold. The black people working in town have to get up very early to cover the long distance to town. All along the coast there is a network of footpaths coming together to form a single path into town.

Approximately every three kilometres the man who is first on the way makes a little fire in the path to chase away the cold from his body. Before he continues his journey he adds some fuel to keep the fire going for the man coming after him. Thus this chain action is kept up until the last man has passed – a moving manifestation of neighbourly love and service.

When our family members need one another, one will ask another to add some fuel to the fire. Then we know that we need to pray compassionately for one another, think about one another and do whatever we can to help.

One night while I was out fishing, I misjudged the weather and was unexpectedly overcome by the winter cold on the rocks – wearing nothing but shorts and a short-sleeved shirt. In spite of a very successful night of fishing I was frozen to the bone before daybreak.

One of the black men sitting by the fire took his blanket from his shoulders and draped it over my back and legs. Notwithstanding my protestations he insisted that he didn't need the blanket as much as I did: "You see, Umfundisi, you cannot creep into the fire like we do. Your eyes cannot bear the smoke."

Of all the kind actions done to me in all my life, this was one of the most considerate and I shall be thankful for it all through my life. I want to add that it was also one of the actions most inspired by Scripture, because it was loving, unselfish and sincere: reminiscent of Somebody else who came to cover us in his blood so that we could survive.

We in our sophisticated society often have so many hidden motives for doing something good for someone else, that we sometimes need a cold night on the rocks of the Transkei coast to teach us the real meaning of unselfish loving-kindness: a kind deed done by someone who doesn't know us and of whom we do not expect it.

EIGHT

THOUGHTS ON FATHER'S DAY

On Father's Day a dad may surely rightfully claim a turn to speak. For this reason I dare to write this open letter to mothers in the name of a great number of fathers. Most likely mothers will not always agree with my opinions, but even if it is only a stimulus to wider discussion it will be reward enough.

Many of us who are fathers today grew up in a period when there were established perceptions about the role of the father in the family. He had to be a macho man with a "cowboys don't cry" philosophy. He never wore his feelings on his sleeve and seldom showed his love – and when he did, definitely not in public.

For this reason, many of today's fathers find that hard work and difficult adjustments are needed to satisfy the demands that contemporary society makes on a father. The old view of the father as role model is woven into the texture of the thoughts and deeds of many of us, and it is not easy to get rid of it.

However, with the help of understanding mothers we have progressed quite a long way.

Do not lose courage or become impatient with us. Sometimes we still stumble in our new and unaccustomed role. We are trying hard, but it is not always easy.

Together with you we will work at it and be victorious.

Already it is easier for many of us to tell our wives, "I do love you ... " and to mean it sincerely. We have discovered how all-important hearing these words is to you, and the time will come when we shall say it to you easily and regularly. We do love you and we think you know it. However, because you are women, you need to hear it often.

Those days are irrevocably past when we could lightly dispose of this need by saying, "On our wedding day I told you I love you. Whenever I change my mind, I'll let you know." We are glad those days are past, and we shall exert ourselves to pronounce our love regularly and with sincerity.

On Father's Day we only ask: give us opportunity, give us reason, and give us love too. Women do not have the exclusive right to declarations of love. Even though it doesn't always seem like it, we can also not live without it.

Another matter arising from the heart: maintain your femininity. True, you are our equals and in many respects our superiors. There is no sphere of life that you cannot enter, and you invariably do so gracefully and successfully, regardless of whether in sports, culture, law, science, social services, politics, or religion.

You introduce a fresh dimension in every sphere of life. You are extremely suitable to be judges, scientists, leaders in society and culture, premiers and moderators – but please stay feminine. Your femininity is what makes you unique, and for that reason Scripture says that the all-wise Creator created us "man and woman."

In our diversity there are many blessings for humankind. There are ineradicable differences between us, which we have to honour. Men cannot bear children AND we cannot suckle babies, even as women do not shave or become bald. In the final instance we want to be married to the "woman" who, before marriage, sent delicious electrical shocks through our bodies and made us go weak at the knees by merely looking in our direction.

After the wedding you must remain just as careful of your femininity as before. Remain attentive to the enhancement of your natural beauty, to weight control, neatness and charm. A tracksuit is a wonderful garment … but do not live in it.

In doing so you will ensure that we as fathers will always and in all situations remain aware and appreciative of your beauty and charm. Do not display your charm and winsomeness only when there are visitors, but every day when the two of us have to face life's challenges together. You will never know how much it means to us.

Another delicate matter: for the best part of

married life mothers are busy raising children and being homemakers. Many of you also do welfare service or follow a highly specialised career. It happens so easily that we live past each other – even though it might sound like a cliché. For this reason we must make special time for each other in the midst of all these demands.

Once the children have left home and the nest is empty, only the two of us will remain. Then we might realise that we have been so busy with less important matters, which lie at the periphery of our love, that our relationship has become dull. Then we may not have anything more to say to or do for each other. That will be a disaster.

Let us give each other space and let us not claim each other in selfish love.

Each of us needs his or her own support group. Let us trust each other, because distrust undermines a relationship, whereas trust refines and enriches it.

Do not regard these Father's Day thoughts as criticism, but as sincere requests from the hearts of fathers. Thank you that you make a peaceful home for us. Thank you for all your unsung deeds of love; for all the things you are and which only you can be because you were created as women. May you always stay the woman of our spring love. And thank you in anticipation for the delicious breakfast, the flowers and the declaration of love which we'll get while still in bed on Father's Day!

BUT I WILL SING OF
YOUR STRENGTH, IN
THE MORNING I WILL
SING OF YOUR LOVE

PSALM 59:16

NINE

—*—*—*—*—

THE DONKEY COMMANDO

One of the saddest and most troublesome problems in a children's home is children who run away. They simply take to the road or secretly hop on a train at night. After a few days they are brought back by the police, hungry and in a battered condition, and often unjustly stigmatised as criminals.

Often, however, it was not the naughtiest children who ran away, but the intelligent and well-behaved ones. They seldom planned to go home to their parents. On the contrary, life in the children's home gave them greater security and often more love than the home from which they had had to be removed.

Gradually it came to light that the running away was directly connected to the adventurousness of the children. Let us confess without reproach: the old children's homes were often regarded as reformatories, fenced in with sturdy barbed wire, with bars before every window and little freedom to move around. There was no outlet for the natural adventurousness of the children.

They must have felt as if they were living in a jail where there was absolutely no space for imagination and liberty. The only adventure left to them was to run away.

We put our heads together and made some radical changes. The barbed wire fences were removed, the bars before the windows were taken down and greater freedom of movement was allowed. Weekend camps and holiday excursions were organised to give the children a change of environment and space for satisfying their adventurousness.

A camping ground at Port St. Johns on the Transkei coast was obtained and the children were taken there on every possible occasion. These changes brought about surprising and unexpected results.

Runaways became a very rare exception. The children's collective opinion about running away was changed, and the transgressors soon felt like outcasts to whom we often had to give protection.

The children's performance in school increased in proportion to the satisfaction of their adventurousness, and their general behaviour improved.

****

One of the most encouraging experiments was the "donkey commando."

The children's home at Ugie owned a beautiful farm about eight kilometres out of town. There was a lot of unused pasture on the farm. One of our adventure projects was to buy donkeys, keep them on the farm during the week and then put them to use for the children during weekends.

All the practical and logistical problems were overcome: pasture was created at the children's home, fodder was transported from the farm and a water supply was constructed. The full co-operation of the farm manager, Andries Roodt, was obtained.

The privilege of "owning" a donkey for the weekend was related to achievement in school-work and exemplary behaviour during the week. Furthermore, every child who had earned a donkey had to care for it him or herself.

The donkeys had to be bought at auctions held on Wednesday mornings at the village common. I went from auction to auction – even in the neighbouring towns – and bought every suitable donkey.

Soon the farmers in the vicinity heard about the donkey project. When I made a bid on a donkey there was a heavenly silence among the buyers. Nobody made any further bids – to the dismay of the auctioneer and the owner. In this way we obtained thirty-six donkeys cheaply – one even for the ridiculous amount of fifty cents. It was mostly the same farmers who later supplied the donkey commando with fodder and water when the riders were in their neighbourhood.

Every Friday afternoon during dinner the names of the thirty-six chosen ones were read in the different houses. They could then run to the farm to fetch their "weekend donkeys" which were their sole property during that weekend. What a treat it was for the staff and the children every weekend when the team could run to the farm after finishing their homework!

Soon every donkey had its own original name to which it responded. The strengths and caprices of each donkey could be counted on the fingers. Each donkey was also curried, fed and cared for with intense love.

We became increasingly aware that these love-starved children carried a huge amount of love in themselves and only sought somebody or something to shower it upon. For this reason these children later mostly became excellent parents. It is as if they wanted to prevent their children from having to suffer the sorrows they had to endure.

Long ago the Man from Nazareth rode into Jerusalem on a donkey and was joyfully greeted with "Hosanna!" by adults and children alike. The donkey thus played a humble part in our salvation. Thus it was in the children's home for the donkey commando: a simple story with great results.

TEN

—*—*—*—*—

BEARERS OF LOVE

The donkey commando established at the children's home at Ugie was responsible for many an unforgettable incident and became a true blessing in the lives of the children.

The very first weekend of the donkey commando was an unforgettable and exciting experience. On Friday afternoon it was announced that the thirty-six chosen riders could ride on the road to Elliot the next day.

"How far?" they all wanted to know. "As far as you want to ride. The only condition is that you have to be home by sundown. Auntie Louise will supply sandwiches and cold drinks for each of you."

A deadly silence reigned. Then the question lying unspoken in all hearts was asked by a cynic who hadn't earned a donkey for this weekend: "Aren't you afraid that they'll run away?"

"I trust them," was the only thing I could answer.

Many of the older staff members were also sceptical. It is difficult for some people to get rid of deeply rooted perceptions, especially in the case of such a radical change. Wide-eyed they whispered audibly, "Now they are even supplied with transport … as well as provisions." This was nothing less than looking for trouble, they thought.

Early on Saturday morning the riders were getting ready to depart, while those staying home jealously looked on. However, when they departed in a cloud of dust an earsplitting cheer went up – as if they were Attila's Huns departing on a raid. The riders sat adroitly on their donkeys and we were pleasantly surprised by the quick pace maintained by the donkeys up the hill on the way to the station.

Little did we know of the slightly warmed pebbles, which the riders' friends had had to push in under the tails of the donkeys. The poor animals then gripped the pebbles with their tails and it made them run as if they had a tiger in the tank! It wasn't long before they disappeared over the horizon.

Only then a vague but gnawing uncertainty crept upon Louise and me. We looked at each other with the unspoken question in our eyes: "What if they don't come back?" Much later we secretly kept an eye on the station hill to see whether they weren't returning yet. Later it was three o' clock … four o' clock … and at last five o' clock. No sign of a single donkey or rider.

Our hearts sank into our shoes. Staff members were looking at us with reproachful eyes that clearly said, "We warned you!"

The sun was going down and we kept on looking hopefully towards the station hill.

Then the first donkey and its rider appeared, but the rider was walking next to the donkey. One by one they appeared over the brow of the hill, all next to their donkeys. When they approached, we saw they were all walking uncomfortably wide-legged, but without exception with a glorious expression in their eyes!

The sores or "crowns" where their backsides had connected with the hard spines of the donkeys were painful, but it had been a day of days nonetheless. Never would the thirty-six riders ever forget it; never would the others stop asking questions and discussing it.

Everybody was home and a new era had dawned. In a children's home, as in all other homes, a hiding is often the easiest solution for dealing with a disobedient child. With a little more exertion we can make alternative plans – sometimes with surprising results.

That evening thirty-six exhausted, sore, but happy boys were standing in a long row while Louise tenderly treated the sore places with ointment and love. Unbelievably, they stood there and enjoyed the soft touch.

One little one turned around and told Louise with complete honesty while she was busy with him, "Aunty, up to now I have only been touched with a cane there." His eyes were shining with suppressed tears. The longing for a tender touch was overwhelming, and here somebody was lovingly touching their backsides!

Things were never the same in that children's

home. Again the donkeys were unwitting bearers of love, like so many years before. They became a strong link between the children and us and produced loyal love. After this those boys would willingly have gone through fire for Louise. Runaways became a thing of the past.

The donkeys had another spin-off. They taught the children in a normal and practical way about love, sex, birth and life. I still get a lump in my throat when I think about how protective they were towards Sheila after I had explained to them that she was going to be a mother. If somebody wanted trouble for himself he would only have to try and ride her late in her pregnancy. They pampered and spoilt her terribly.

Shortly before Sheila gave birth I had to undergo an eye operation. I had to lie at home in a darkened room with bandages over my eyes to recuperate. One morning an ear-splitting din broke loose in the house. A knot of children burst into the room and all of them spoke together excitedly: "Look, Uncle, this is Bambi, Sheila's foal!" When they realised I couldn't see, they described Bambi in the finest detail.

Just as well that my eyes were bandaged. Thus the children couldn't see the tears of gratitude welling up in my eyes unstoppably. When at last they were gone and the quiet had returned, I whispered softly, "Thank you, great Friend of children and Master, thank you for what you have come to teach our children through the donkeys."

ELEVEN

—*—*—*—*—

THE LONGEST JOURNEY

People go to surprisingly much trouble to adorn, improve and beautify their bodies. They spend hours at the hairdresser, the manicurist and the dressmaker; they apply make-up painfully correctly and precisely; they choose their clothes with care; they do strenuous exercises to keep it fit and healthy.

Thus we can continue to list examples of how people go to great lengths to take care of their exterior.

No fault can be found with this. On the contrary, it is extremely important for you to be attractive, fit, well-clothed and neat. However, man consists of two components: body and spirit, external and internal. Both require equal attention if you wish to be a balanced, complete and mature person.

Dag Hammarskjöld, former secretary-general of the United Nations, said, "Man's longest journey is the journey to his deepest inner being."

We must regularly undertake this journey to investigate our inner being. Only in this way can you discern whether your internal growth is keeping pace with your external. The real danger is that your external life might be satisfactory but your internal life miserable.

The Man of Nazareth told the church people of his time, "You clean the outside of the cup and dish, but inside they are full of greed and self-indulgence. First clean the inside of the cup and dish, and then the outside will also be clean."

You must work dedicatedly to beautify and ennoble your inner surroundings. In truth, you *choose* your own inner world: you can choose to live in a desert or in a paradise. If you have become shallow, dry and brittle inwardly, the desert will creep up centimetre by centimetre to occupy your inner world.

However, with a little bit of effort and the grace from Above you can create an inner paradise that will give a special dimension to your life. In addition, everybody with whom you associate will be eager to visit this oasis in order to share in this paradise.

Elsa was a pupil in my Afrikaans class during her final year in school. After many years I recently met her again – the same sunny, spontaneous and friendly person of long ago. We discussed our wellbeing, our family and common friends, and then I asked her how her reading was doing.

"No, Sir, the last books I read were our prescribed books in matric."

And I went to so much trouble trying to induce a love of reading!

This saddened me immeasurably: on the one hand because I had failed in my calling as a teacher, and on the other because of the inner poverty that she certainly must be experiencing in her life. If you live in a desert, you inevitably draw all your companions into the desert with you.

How does one enrich and ennoble one's inner surroundings so that one becomes a paradise person? Naturally also by reading timeless, immortal, universal literature.

When last have you read poetry and felt touched by it? When last have you succumbed to a great piece of music, drinking it into your spirit, your mind, and your emotions, knowing that you are a better person for having listened to it? When last have you risen early to watch the sunrise and become conscious of the greatness of God? Or undertaken an excursion into nature or in a garden and experienced the presence of God tangibly? Or gone to see a good movie, opera or other performance?

There are also the gifts of grace that God has given us to enrich our inner world: the conversation with him that we call prayer – not only talking to him, but also listening to him; keeping ourselves busy with the eternal Word's wisdom, directions, comfort, encouragement, poetry and prose; the sensible conversation with kindred spirits bringing with it unparalleled enrichment.

Paul told the church in Philippi, and through them also us: … *whatever is true, whatever is noble, whatever is right, whatever is pure, whatever is lovely, whatever is admirable – if anything is excellent or praiseworthy – think about such things* (Phil. 4:8).

Paradise people are the givers of this kind of life. Desert people are grabbers who take everything out of life with white knuckles and clenched fists and give nothing back.

The givers give of their beautiful inner selves without expecting anything in return. Through the eyes of such people God smiles upon this world.

Do undertake an inward journey to make an honest evaluation of your inner surroundings. It may be a life-altering experience, especially if you reach out to him who said, *"I am making everything new!"* (Rev. 21:5).

THE LORD'S LOVINGKINDNESS INDEED NEVER CEASE, FOR HIS COMPASSIONS NEVER FAIL. THEY ARE NEW EVERY MORNING.

LAMENTATIONS 3:22-23 (NAS)

TWELVE

—*—*—*—*—

SAY THANK YOU ... BEFORE IT'S TOO LATE!

During the first year of his ministry a student in theology who had just completed his studies wrote three letters of thanks to people from his childhood – people who had had a positive and formative influence on his life and thoughts.

He received answers from all three people. On reading them he was deeply touched and was brought to a new awareness of the profound influence of those two little words: "thank you."

The first letter was written to Aunt Lettie Roos, who was his substitute mother when he ended up in the children's home in Ugie. For the first sixteen years of his life she was the only mother he knew.

From her he learnt about the good things in life; he learnt to love and appreciate the beauty of nature; he developed an appreciation for good music and a passionate love for flowers; he learnt to love poetry and literature. As ex-teacher she was a competent educator. For all these things and much more he tried to thank her and tell her what they meant to him in his life.

In the letter he received in return from her, she said that his letter had made her deeply joyful and thankful. She told how she missed Uncle Gys, her deceased husband, and how comfortlessly lonely it sometimes was in the old-age home.

His letter was the first one she had ever received from any of her foster children. In the space of thirty-five years she had given more than two thousand children a footing in life. She told how surprised she had been that he remembered the poetry and the flowers and the beauty of nature. She had thought that the digging, the making of flower-beds, the weeding and watering of the small plants with a watering-can, the debudding of carnation and aster plants had only been drudgery to him. It warmed her heart to know that it had brought him so much joy.

She thanked him for all the good things he had said in his letter. She had not realised how much he had appreciated her love. She remembered him as a little curly-haired boy who came sleepily to their bed on cold winter mornings after the other children had risen. He would crawl in at the foot of the bed and enjoy another half an hour of sleep, cosy in their bed. She remembered how she came specially to give him a goodnight kiss and thought he was ashamed of it in front of the other boys. She was overjoyed to know that he did appreciate it and was remembering it.

If only substitute mothers could know how much of a child's sorrow they ease just by being there to fulfil the longing for parents. It is so seldom expressed. That was the beginning of regular correspondence between those two until the time when he had to drive to Jamestown to bury Aunt Lettie next to Uncle Gys Roos.

The second letter he wrote was to the most unforgettable teacher he had ever known, a teacher in whose class he had been from standard 4 to standard 6 at the intermediate school in Ugie. Mr. Albert Steward had been his role model and hero all through the years: on the rugby or hockey fields; on the tennis court or in the swimming pool; in the symphony orchestra that Mr. Gustav Pheil with great trouble managed to get together in the small town; as a singer of stature – and as his spiritual mentor. This was the man who had led him step by step over a period of more than a year to the greatest experience of his life: becoming a reborn Christian.

His widow answered the letter: Mr. Steward had gone to meet his Maker. The young minister had not been aware that his teacher had married after leaving Ugie, just as he had also not known that he had died.

In her letter she thanked the minister for all the good things he had mentioned in his letter and confirmed that everything had remained true up to end of Mr. Steward's life. The young minister was very sorry that he had postponed his letter of appreciation until it was too late.

His third letter was to Mr. Bucky William Hope, the trustworthy, humble and dedicated secretary of the children's home. He came from England with a calling to work among orphans. He had a burning interest in theology. His library would make any minister green with envy. This man with his goatee and stately bearing was one of the people who had had a formative influence on the young minister.

In his single bedroom with the smell of paraffin, condensed milk, books and sheets of paper covered in writing they conversed hours on end about the calling of the young minister.

He received an answer to his letter, not from Mr. Hope – but from the director of the children's home. He had taken the liberty to open the letter and read it. Mr. Hope had died a number of months before on his knees before his bed. He died as he had lived: facing his Master.

The young minister cried shamelessly when he read the letter and mourned Mr. Hope for a long time. From then onwards the young minister made thanking an integral part of his life.

Every time when he visits Ugie he goes to the humble graveyard and the tombstone that the children's home had had erected on the grave of Mr. Hope. And every time he realises anew that it is better to say thank you while people are still alive, rather than to cry warm tears beside a cold granite tombstone.

THIRTEEN

—*—*—*—*—

TO HARBOUR ANGELS

Disaster and tragedy have blighted our country as much as they have any country in the world. The Cape of Storms has always been true to its name. It has seen shipwrecks and loss of life, oil-besmirched penguins and beaches. Flood damage to houses and property has been fearsome and tragic. Add to this bush fires, losses of stock and terrible winter cold, with snow, frost, and icy temperatures.

We see all these events on television, read about them in the papers, and hear about them on the radio. We hear about homeless people without refuge, tramps, the unemployed, the needy. For most of us it is very convenient: we can help those nameless, addressless, faceless needy people by a donation to an organisation.

A few dispensable tins of food (perhaps hoarded before the elections), one or two threadbare blankets, useless old clothes and a few rands' worth of groceries ... With these we can soothe our consciences and sit cosily and warmly in front of our television sets and fireplaces, or snuggle into bed on our electric blankets. Conveniently we can forget about the tramp or unemployed person who is trying to sleep under an old newspaper on a park bench in our smart neighbourhood, or about little children who die of exposure, cold, disease and hunger in the arms of powerless parents.

Do we really care? Do we care to the extent that our compassion means personal involvement with a person in need? Somebody with a name, a face, an address? It would make such a great difference.

Thus it was in the case of Stephen Foster. Stephen Foster was the writer of more than two hundred popular melodies and lyrics that are still living on in the hearts of millions. Some of the most well known the reader will recognise: "Beautiful dreamer," "Jeanie with the light brown hair," "Old folks at home," "My old Kentucky home," "Oh, Susannah!" and "Camptown races."

His last years were a sad contrast to his earlier life. Because of his abuse of alcohol his life gradually deteriorated until he landed in the Bowery – the twilight world of New York's tramps and drunkards. One night he was taken to the Bellevue hospital nearby as one of the hundreds of charity admissions. Nobody knew who he was and apparently nobody cared.

How he had ended up in an unconscious state in that third class hospital on that dreary morning and what had happened to him were covered in shrouds of disinterest. The overburdened nurses saw him as just another case.

His cheap overnight lodgings in the Bowery cost him twenty-five cents per night. The rooms were utterly dismal. Like many of the inhabitants Foster lived mainly on drink. His health was impaired and he was dying.

On that cold morning before the first cheering rays of the sun crept over New York, Foster – a caricature of the man he had once been, looking twice his age – stumbled to a washbasin, slipped in his drunken condition and fell. The basin was ripped from the wall and shattered on the cement floor. He fell on top of the shards. He was found in a heap of shards with a deep cut in his throat and serious injuries to his forehead.

A doctor was called and stopped the bleeding temporarily with a coarse black thread – good enough for someone from the Bowery. For most of them it was, as was generally believed, a last station on the way to the mortuary. The only thing that the dying tramp pleaded for was a drink. A fellow tramp shared the dregs from a bottle of rum with him.

Foster was transferred to the Bellevue hospital where he lay for three days without being able to eat ... and at last he died, totally unknown.

A friend who came to look for him was referred to the mortuary. There he was identified. When they gathered his meagre possessions together there was only a ragged military coat with twenty-five cents in one pocket and a scrap of paper in the other. That was all that he possessed on earth: twenty-five cents to pay for one more night's stay in the Bowery and a scrap of paper with these words written on it: "Dear friends and gentle people." Somebody remarked that it sounded like the words of a song.

However, who cared? Perhaps it was an unborn song in the heart of this onetime genius who died so tragically when he was thirty-eight years old – Stephen Foster, the man who induced the people of his time to sing; the man for whom nobody really cared.

The writer of the letter to the Hebrews said: *Do not forget to entertain strangers, for by so doing some people have entertained angels without knowing it* (Heb. 13:2).

Some of them will not look like angels. Perhaps they will look like tramps, but it is possible that there is a song in their heart, which may die if nobody really cares.

We are sophisticated: we know all the excuses we can use to justify our decision not to become personally involved. We know how convenient it is to refer the needy to the state, the church and charity organisations.

However, our Master on occasion spoke about charity to the hungry and the thirsty, to strangers and jailbirds, to the needy and sick. He said: *"Whatever you did for the least of these brothers of mine, you did for me"* (Mt. 25:40).

FOURTEEN

—*—*—*—*—

NEW SPRING, FRESH LIFE

The arrival of spring awakens a wealth of sensations and thoughts in all of us. Nature speaks to us in its own unique language. The Dutch poet Guido Gezelle rightly said: "If the soul listens, nature speaks in a language that lives."

In the Boland spring comes suddenly and with breathtaking beauty.

Suddenly you perceive new life all around you. The trees look like gigantic bouquets and proudly exhibit their beautiful flowers. The world is transformed into a fairytale landscape.

New life in all its green youthfulness burgeons on all sides: *"See! The winter is past; the rains are over and gone. Flowers appear on the earth; the season of singing has come"* (Song 2:11-12).

Thus each year spring brings us the message of renewal, of new life, of new growth. We are lifted out of our mouldy winter ruts of drudgery and routine, and placed amidst a new awakening and new visions.

Suddenly we have the urge to fulfil our

dreams. One can renounce one's dreams so easily. Sören Kierkegaard (1813-1855), a Danish theologian and philosopher, wrote an allegory about renounced dreams:

A flock of wild ducks were on their way to the north to escape the cold winter in the south. When they were about halfway, one of them looked down on the backyard of a farmer's cottage and saw a coop with a number of domesticated ducks. He decided to go down for a while, take a drink of water and let his tired wings rest ... and then he would continue the journey.

The food was so good, the coop so safe, and the companionship so amicable that he decided to linger for a day.

The day became a week and the week a month. He enjoyed the comfortable life on the farm and decided to wait for the next flock of wild ducks and join them instead.

When they flew past high in the air he flapped his wings, fluttered slowly, and rose ... But he got no higher than the bottom part of the roof and then plunged down into the coop again. The good food and the peaceful life had made him fat and lazy.

No matter, he comforted himself, when the flock returns home, I shall fly with them.

His stay with the tame ducks was easy and relaxed. When the call of the wild ducks high up in the air on their flight to the south sounded, a strange longing was aroused in his heart. He badly wanted to join them, but due to his comfortable life he could hardly lift himself off the ground.

Just you wait, he reassured himself again, next year I'll be flying with you. And so it went season after season: every time when he heard the call high up in the air the terrible longing and strong determination were there, but every time he postponed it for the sake of the comfortable and cosy life.

And then, one day, when the wild ducks were flying past high up in the air, he didn't even hear them any more ...

*****

Spring with its strangely captivating call comes again and tells us anew: you dare not forsake your dreams. There is no man so spiritually bankrupt that he has no dream.

However, it doesn't help simply to be idle dreamers: we have to soar up and beyond with the wings of faith and fulfil those dreams through effort and determination.

We must courageously accept the challenges inevitably brought about by our dreams. Place a sword in the hand of your dreams and fight until you have conquered all difficulties and realised your dreams.

The American theologian Carl Schurz said ideals are like the stars: we cannot reach them, but like the seafarer we chart our life's course according to them.

There is only one exciting thing to do with a dream or an ideal: fulfil and materialise it.

To dream faithfully, to hitch the chariot of your life to a star, is the first piece of equipment needed for the struggle of life. Your dreams are the golden ladder that you climb to the high places in life. They bring you to the mountaintops from where you can glimpse the distant land to which you are travelling.

Dreams are the shining lamp that lights your way through the dark valley. Your dreams are the inner flame that gives you the strength and energy for the struggle of life.

Without dreams, spring dreams that flare up brightly every now and again, one's life falls back into a rut. And a rut is but a shallow grave.

Spring reminds us that the Creator blesses us with a new opportunity.

Spring demonstrates that nature takes hold of that opportunity and lets the best in her come to the fore in:

- pupils and students in their studies;
- mothers in their homemaking task;
- the farmer in his labour;
- the politician in the national housekeeping;
- the teacher in his teaching; and
- the minister in his preaching and pastoral work.

Everyone – in every sphere of life – has this spring opportunity for new, sparkling life.

Spring teaches us in a dramatic way that from stagnation new life can come forth; from death, bubbling new life; from mediocrity, excellence.

As a bonus we get the beauty of spring, a beauty that pulses in your heart when you see it.

May this spring be beautiful for you.

May it be a renewed and fulfilled inspiration to chase after your dream again until you find it.

FIFTEEN

—*—*—*—*—

BRING HEAVEN INTO YOUR SOUL

Faith is an anchor connecting you to God, an anchor that prevents your life from falling apart. According to the unknown writer of the letter to the Hebrews sincere faith is … *being sure of what we hope for and certain of what we do not see* (Heb. 11:1).

Isaiah said: … *but those who hope in the LORD will renew their strength. They will soar on wings like eagles; they will run and not grow weary, they will walk and not be faint* (Is. 40:31).

However, in addition to "true faith" there are also various false variants. There is *historic faith,* which is merely rational agreement with the great truths of Scripture; *temporary faith* or *simulated faith,* which is an emotional welling up that lasts but a short while; and *miracle faith,* which only has appreciation for the miraculous and the supernatural. Perhaps the most common form of false faith is *superstition.* Superstition means that you add something to true faith to try and strengthen it, because your faith is not strong enough. It is a prop to support your faith, but it is unreliable, gives way in a crisis and time and again leaves you scarlet with shame.

History offers many examples of mass-superstition. One of the most striking is the one arising from the plague called the "Black Death," which struck England in 1664.

It was called the Black Death for two reasons. Firstly, the bodies of the victims turned dark with black spots all over the skin. Secondly, dark ignorance veiled the cause of the disease, and consequently there was no way to control it.

Approximately twenty-five million people died before the epidemic was stopped. A few cases occurred in May 1664, but were ignored. A year later in May 560 people died; by June there were 6 137; in July more than 17 000 and in August 31 000.

Panic broke loose. Two thirds of the British population evacuated their homes to try and escape death. Needless to say, superstition raged like an uncontrollable fire. Somebody somewhere made the foolish remark that bad air was the cause of the disease.

As a result people began carrying flower petals in their pockets and superstitiously believed (and hoped) that the fragrance of the flower petals would prevent the disease.

Groups of sick people who were still able to walk were taken out of their hospital rooms to gardens. While holding hands they walked around in circles in the gardens while inhaling deeply the aroma of the flowers.

When patients were not able to leave their beds, doctors filled their pockets with brightly coloured posies. When they visited a patient, they moved around the bed and scattered the posies over him or her.

Another superstitious action was added to the list of supposed cures for the disease. Many people believed that if the bad air in the lungs could be expelled it would save the patient. Consequently they placed ashes in a spoon and brought it near the nose of the dying person. This caused a mighty sneeze, which would presumably then cleanse the lungs.

However, neither the petals nor the ashes could ward off death. There was no hope before the true cause was discovered: the bite of fleas living on infected rats.

From these superstitions a children's game which is still played today was born. According to tradition the song accompanying the game was first heard from a ragged old man who was pushing the corpses of victims in a cart through the streets of London, on his way to the mortuary. Readers probably know the song from childhood – in a somewhat different version: "Ring around the roses, a pocket full of posies, ashes, ashes, we all fall down!"

Superstition causes us to feel unsafe and fearful – and also powerless in the face of our fears. It is fed by self-fabricated, exaggerated lies that grow so rampantly and out of all proportion, that they hide God himself from us.

Superstition is found in practically every sphere of life. Sportsmen have their unshakeable little superstitions without which they believe they cannot be successful; gamblers have superstitions which ostensibly would help them to win; entertainment stars have superstitions on which they rely during performances; older people are superstitious regarding their health and safety; many mothers have superstitions about the births of their children; businessmen have superstitions when they make deals; millions of people across the world are superstitious about what their horoscopes say.

Some people refuse to get out of bed or leave their houses on Friday the thirteenth, fearing that a disaster will strike them on this day. Many hotels have no room number thirteen. There are innumerable well-known superstitions of this kind.

The height of superstition, however, is often to be found in our religion.

Religious superstition is ruthless tyranny – the many martyrs in Christian history attest to this fact. Superstition makes a slave of you. If anything in your religion has enslaved you it has probably grown from the fertile soil of superstition.

Look earnestly at John 5:1-7 and see how Christ treats the superstition of church people. Your church can become a superstition to you, or your Bible, or even Holy Communion. Our Redeemer came to free us also from any superstition and to lead us to the full truth.

Superstition brings the Black Death of slavery into our religion and life. It may be well meant, but good intentions cannot liberate you. Christ is the One who liberates you. Your superstitions may be as well intentioned as those old superstitions regarding a pocket full of posies or a spoonful of ashes. Ultimately, however, your superstitions will amount to nothing more than a song sung by a ragged old man called "Superstition" as he pushes a spiritual corpse through the dismal streets on a cart.

C. H. Spurgeon, that prince of preachers, said: "Small faith will bring your soul in heaven, but great faith will bring heaven into your soul."

THEREFORE WE DO
NOT LOSE HEART ...
INWARDLY WE ARE
BEING RENEWED DAY
BY DAY. SO WE FIX
OUR EYES ... ON WHAT
IS UNSEEN. FOR WHAT
IS SEEN IS TEMPORARY,
BUT WHAT IS
UNSEEN IS ETERNAL.

LAMENTATIONS 3:22-23 (NAS)

SIXTEEN

—*—*—*—*—

FAITH CAN NEVER EXPECT TOO MUCH

Soutaar is the inherited farm of Chris and Hetta van Rensburg. It lies between Britstown and Prieska, and here Chris and Hetta farm the land, assisted by Andries, their son, and Michele, their daughter-in-law.

Let it be said without doubt or hesitation: Chris and Hetta are true church people who play an indispensable part in the mother congregation of the Dutch Reformed Church, as well as in the mission church of Britstown.

This introduction is intended only to explain why the two ministers of the two different congregations, Michiel Fourie and Nico Kriek, both receive an annual invitation to come and shoot a springbok for the parsonage every year.

Thus it happened this year again.

This hunting story is about Reverend Nico.

Even Reverend Nico will agree to the fact that he can by no means be called a Nimrod when it comes to hunting. His achievements on the hunting ground have always been more than modest. This was his third hunt, and he had always come away with empty hands.

I do not know whether his heart is truly in the hunt. His passionate love for animals is only exceeded by his love for his beautiful wife, Elna. And about Elna's love for animals an omnibus can be written. She tames everything: meerkats, hedgehogs, birds, and, yes, even a rock-rabbit that uses the toilet.

However, Reverend Nico would never decline an invitation to shoot a springbok – he loves biltong too much.

The team who went hunting on that day were the ministers Michiel and Nico, Le Roux van Tonder of Malmesbury and of course Chris and Andries. They went in bakkies, which had facilities to maintain radio contact with the house.

Hetta especially wanted Reverend Nico to shoot his first springbok on that day. Her tender heart couldn't even bear imagining his embarrassment if he didn't succeed.

Hetta has a watertight solution to every problem she encounters: she prays. In between the messages she received per radio from the bakkies she prayed fervently that Reverend Nico would succeed.

At the first encounter with the springboks everybody was successful, except Reverend Nico. He did fire two shots, but both missed.

This induced Hetta to call on a guest from Malmesbury, Mali Badenhorst, to support her in praying. Together they prayed earnestly.

In mitigation of Reverend Nico's case it should be said that his gun compared unfavourably with the sophisticated weapons of the other men. They had the very best hunting rifles, costing between R2 000 and R3 000 each and equipped with telescopes and all the other tricks of the trade, making it practically impossible to miss a shot. He used an old Lee Enfield 303 mark 4 that he had bought for R36 at an auction of obsolete army equipment. He shot with ordinary steel point military cartridges while the other men used soft-nosed bullets specially designed for hunting. And don't assume that Reverend Nico was a bad shot. With an R1-rifle he was one of the best riflemen in the commando.

The day proceeded, and when after the second volley Hetta had to hear that Reverend Nico was still unsuccessful, she called up reinforcements: the help of grandma Katie van Rensburg of the old age home's prayer group was requested and they prayed with renewed diligence for Reverend Nico.

Chris was just as eager for Reverend Nico to succeed. He dropped him behind a hill where the fence formed an angle. The horse riders who did the hustling had to try and drive the bucks in a corner so that Reverend Nico could get an easy shot.

He was dropped at a shrub with the order to sit absolutely still until the bucks were within range.

Contrary to all hunting protocol Reverend Nico was not dressed in hunting clothes that would camouflage him. Clothed in blue denim trousers and a bright blue tracksuit jacket he was sitting behind the shrub, sucking calmly on a bright yellow orange, waiting for the bucks.

No buck appeared within view.

Suddenly, however, he heard a rustling sound behind him, like that of the feet of buck on stones. When he turned around very slowly a buck was standing on the hill 125 metres from him.

He aimed carefully, pulled the trigger and saw the buck fall down. He walked to where the buck was lying. To his utter amazement he saw two bucks lying there, each with a neat bullet wound through the neck. This is the unvarnished truth, not any old hunting tale!

When Chris, who had heard the single shot, arrived on the scene and saw the two bucks, he couldn't believe his eyes! Only then did Reverend Nico hear about the trio who were praying for him so earnestly and with such heartfelt commitment.

He dryly commented, "Chris, can't we go and look at the place where I missed the first two bucks? If people were praying so earnestly it is possible that there could be another dead buck somewhere."

How true is the old hymn: "Never can faith expect too much."

SEVENTEEN

—*—*—*—*—

THE DARK GRINDSTONE OF SORROW

What is the purpose and meaning of suffering and sorrow? Suffering is a part of our human experience about which only a fool would dare speak thoughtlessly. Therefore, I voice my thoughts on this matter hesitatingly and with the prayer that what I say here will mean something to somebody somewhere.

In his poem "Werktuigkundige" (the title means "mechanic" or "engineer") the Afrikaans poet S. J. Pretorius speaks about suffering:

> Die lewe gaan sy kringloop op die swart
> bank van die ewigheid, God druk die hart
> versigtig daarop vas en slyp dit met
> die donker, skerp klein helsteen van die smart.

Literally translated this means:

Life runs its circle on the black
bench of eternity. God presses the heart
carefully down on it and grinds it with
the dark, sharp grindstone of sorrow.

No human being, no matter how young, how strong or how old, has a safeguard against suffering and sorrow: it is universal. It can come as a gradual process into your life, or it can suddenly and unexpectedly bear down on you like a team of runaway horses.

The question is not whether there will be suffering in your life, but how you will handle it when it comes; whether you will have the inner spiritual strength to survive it.

The philosopher Viktor Frankl said about suffering: "All words are too few and a single word too many to describe suffering."

Job said that suffering forced him to remain silent before God: *Then Job answered the LORD, "I am unworthy – how can I reply to you? I put my hand over my mouth. I spoke once, but I have no answer – twice, but I will say no more"* (Job 40:3-4).

Job lived through shattering experiences: he lost all his children and possessions at once, and simultaneously he lost his health. But his faith made him say in that dark night: *"Shall we accept good from God and not trouble?"* (Job 2:10). This is not fatalism; this is pure, crystallised faith.

We read in Scripture that Jesus himself struggled with the meaning of suffering in Gethsemane. He was sorrowful and troubled and revealed his anguish to his disciples; his sweat became like blood. Nevertheless, his final pronouncement was: *"… Yet not as I will but as you will"* (Mt. 26:39).

It is only God's grace that can help us to conquer and accept suffering and the decline and deterioration of old age. Sometimes we can do nothing to change our circumstances, but we can still glorify God in them.

Suffering is the one thing that can break you on the torture rack; that can spoil the fun of life. Because we have lost paradise through rebellion and disobedience, sorrow and suffering came to live with us. Suffering makes you dependent and vulnerable to the superlative degree, and in the last instance it robs you of your identity.

You can try to disregard suffering by assuming a stoic stance towards it; you can try to explain it away; you can try to camouflage it and give it all kinds of euphemistic names. However, try as you might, suffering cannot just be wished away, hidden or explained away.

Suffering that is faithfully lived through transforms you into another person.

You learn to continually trust that the sunshine will break through the dark night. It gives a new meaning to your life; to yesterday, today and tomorrow.

All of us know the clichés and rhetorical

questions that people ask during times of bitter suffering:

- "Where is God when it hurts?"
- "Does God really care for me?"
- "How can a loving God allow such a thing?"

These are perfectly natural, human questions, which occasionally also arise in the heart of the believer. You have to listen carefully to get an answer to them.

The gospel speaks first about a cross and then about a crown; first about Gethsemane and then about the triumph of the empty grave.

In our suffering the suffering of the Man of Sorrows speaks to us clearly.

The French poet Paul Claudel sees it like this: "God did not come to remove suffering; God did not come to deny suffering, but to fill it with his presence." If you can say that through your suffering God has become a reality to you, that you have come nearer to him because of your sorrow, then your suffering has by no means been just a loss.

The theologian Ferdinand Deist says the following in his book *Oorstaptyd* (literally translated the title means "crossing time"): "If we are changed in the suffering, if we change our approach to life, can accept the whole of life, good and bad, in the pious knowledge that God is there, suffering can also be meaningful."

Mrs. Hauptfleisch was the widow of a minister and had two spastic daughters. When we met her she was eighty years old and her daughters forty-six and forty-four. She dedicated herself to taking care of them every single day, and refused to put them in an institution.

When we asked her how she managed it, she answered, "I grew up on a farm and every Sunday afternoon we went for a walk in the veld with my father and mother. My sister and I were always barefoot. Every time when we came to a thorny patch my mother would pick us up, carry us through the thorns and put us down on the other side.

"When I look at my two daughters, I know: this is my thorny patch! I often feel how the Father picks me up and carries me to the other side."

It is a sublime thing to suffer and still be strong. To procure this strength we must go to the Fountain of strength, so that we may have an anchor during times of suffering. Only if we draw strength from the Father will we reach the other side undamaged, purified and strengthened.

This world has been immeasurably enriched by human suffering. May you add to this wealth in your hour of suffering, because then your suffering will not have been worthless and your life not in vain.

EIGHTEEN

—*—*—*—*—

SET A GUARD BEFORE YOUR MOUTH

The older one gets, the more acutely one realises how scarce trustworthy people are. The longer one lives, the more precious those rare souls who fall in this category become to one.

If I were asked to make a list of characteristics that I regard as essential for somebody occupying a position of trust (be it in management, a governing body, a church board, a cabinet, or a circle of friends), the ability to treat private information confidentially would be very near the top of the list. No leader deserves the respect of people if he or she cannot protect the information that people have given him or her in confidence.

Can you keep a secret? Come now, be as honest as if you were on your deathbed. When privileged information has entered through one of the gates of your senses, does it stay within the walls of your mind ... or is it only a matter of time before a serious leakage occurs?

When gossip reaches you from time to time,

do you refuse to add momentum to it ... or do you encourage it with the help of your uncontrolled tongue? If someone shows trust in you by uttering the following introduction, "What I am going to say now, is absolutely confidential," do you respect the trust put in you? Or do you ignore it by immediately thinking, "What a lovely story to repeat"?

There are four basic rules that apply to anything that you were told in confidence:

- Never repeat what was said to you.
- Do not give way to the temptation to talk.
- Never slander while you are discussing people.
- Never degrade people behind their backs, no matter how much you differ from them.

Our mind can be compared to a graveyard filled with graves, which we should refuse to open. The information in them, no matter how juicy or how dry, must rest in peace in the coffin, sealed to silence under the epitaph: "Told in trust, kept in trust."

Hippocrates, the famous physician of Cos (about 460-377 BC) composed an oath that doctors had to take at the beginning of their career regarding their moral and other obligations. Part of it is: "Whatever I shall hear or see in the course of practising my profession, if it shouldn't be spread, I will never let it leak out, but will maintain such information as sacred secrets."

You and I would not care a jot for a physician who made a habit of letting the secrets of his or her patients leak out. The same is true for a minister, lawyer, teacher, secretary or a trusted friend. Without absolute mutual trust no relationship can grow healthy and strong. No institution in the world of commerce or in education deserves the trust of the public without an administration that is dedicated to the protection of mutual trust.

Information is dynamic and powerful. The person who receives it in trust and then gives it away piece by piece to others, usually does it so that others can be impressed because he or she is supposedly "in the know."

Few things satisfy the ego of the untrustworthy person more than seeing how others listen wide-eyed, while their jaws sag in astonishment. Nothing gives him or her as much pleasure as a listener replying in amazement, "Dear me, I didn't know that! How do you know?"

The wise Solomon wrote sharp words on this matter in the book Proverbs:

- *Wise men store up knowledge, but the mouth of a fool invites ruin* (Prov. 10:14).
- *When words are many, sin is not absent, but he who holds his tongue is wise* (Prov. 10:19).
- *A gossip betrays a confidence, but a trustworthy man keeps a secret* (Prov. 11:13).
- *An evil man is trapped by his sinful talk, but a righteous man escapes trouble* (Prov. 12:13).
- *A gossip betrays a confidence; so avoid a man who talks too much* (Prov. 20:19).
- *Like a bad tooth or a lame foot is reliance on the unfaithful in times of trouble* (Prov. 25:19).

• *Like a city whose walls are broken down is a man who lacks self-control* (Prov. 25:28).

Trustworthiness has to do with the quality of your humanity; with that strength that we call integrity.

We are living in a time in which standards in many spheres are falling, especially in the sphere of morality. Let us be honest with ourselves for once in assessing our position regarding this matter.

Shakespeare let Laertes say to Hamlet: "Be true to yourself, and it must follow as day follows night that then you cannot be untrue to any person."

Be honest: can you keep a secret that was told you in trust?

Then prove it.

JESUS SAID TO HER, "I AM THE RESURRECTION AND THE LIFE. HE WHO BELIEVES IN ME WILL LIVE, EVEN THOUGH HE DIES; AND WHOEVER LIVES AND BELIEVES IN ME WILL NEVER DIE."

JOHN 11:25-26

NINETEEN

—*—*—*—*—

THE FINE, FINE WEB OF THE WORD

Afrikaans should be spoken and written with love. That is the best way – or possibly the only way – to serve the language adequately or to promote its survival. Thus J. Lion Cachet, one of the early Afrikaans language patriots regarded the matter. Thus it was through all the years and thus it will always be.

Every time Afrikaans is spoken and especially when Afrikaans is written we guarantee its survival.

Cachet started what N. P. van Wyk Louw and other great minds later continued. In Cachet's simple poem, "Die Afrikaanse taal" (literally translated the title means "the Afrikaans language"), he mentions the Dutch and French origins of Afrikaans:

> Ek is 'n arme Boerenôi,
> By vele min geag;
> Maar tog is ek van edel bloed,

En van 'n hoog geslag.
Uit Holland het myn pa gekom
Na sonnig Afrika;
Uit Frankryk, waar die druiftros swel,
Myn liewe, mooie ma.

Literally translated this stanza reads:

I am a poor Boer girl
By many scarce esteemed,
But yet I sprung from noble blood
And from an honourable lineage.
My father came from Holland
To sunny Africa;
From France where the grape swells
My dear and lovely mother.

In the last stanza he gives the formula for the survival of the language when he says:

Want ek het onder in myn kis
'n Ware towerstaf,
Wat ek nog van myn ouma het,
En niemand weet daaraf.
Hef ek die staf op: "Moedertaal",
Dan volg die land my na,
En ek is netnou koningin
Van heel Suid-Afrika!

Literally translated this stanza reads:

For at the bottom of my kist

I have a magic wand,
Which I inherited from my grandma,
And nobody knows of it.
I raise the wand: "Mother tongue,"
And all the country follows me,
And soon I will be queen
Of all South Africa!

The Afrikaans language was conceived and born in strife. That it would have to fight for its survival was self-evident from the outset. In his authoritative book *The Great Boer War* Sir Arthur Conan Doyle wrote the following about the people who were mainly responsible for the survival of this beautiful, pulsing, modern language:

> Take a society of Dutch people of the kind who defended themselves for fifty years against the superior power of Spain at a stage when Spain was the most powerful country in the world. Mix this society with the bloodline of those uncompromising French Huguenots who sacrificed hearth and home and fortune and left their fatherland forever when the Edict of Nantes was recalled. It will inevitably result in one of the most stalwart, robust and invincible races ever found on the face of the earth.
>
> Take these formidable people and

> train them for seven generations in unceasing warfare ... in circumstances where no weakling would survive. Give them a lifestyle that forces them to develop extraordinary skill in the use of weapons and in riding, and then give them a country which is extremely suitable for the skills of the hunter, the marksman and the horseman.
>
> Then eventually blend their military abilities with a strict, fatalistic, Old Testament religion and a fiery and consuming patriotism. Combine all these qualities and impulses in one individual and you have the modern Boer: the most formidable opponent ever to cross the path of imperialist Britain.
>
> Our military history mainly consists of our conflict with France, but Napoleon and all his veterans never treated us as roughly as these iron-hard farmers with their antiquated theology and their uncomfortably modern guns.

Therefore it is obvious that all of us who love this language, whatever our lineage or origins might be, will fearlessly speak and write it in order to ensure its survival and growth.

It is not necessary to shout loudly about it, to bedevil human relations because of it, to make forceful demands for it. Instead we should resolutely, in a civilised and dignified way, do what this language demands of us: to speak and to write it. If we do it as gracefully and beautifully as this special language enables us, there is no power on earth that will destroy it.

The history of the language is reflected in the line that runs through from Cachet's "Die Afrikaanse taal" to "Die beiteltjie" (literally translated it means "the little chisel") by N. P. van Wyk Louw:

> Ek kry 'n klein klein beiteltjie,
> ek tik hom en hy klink;
> toe slyp ek en ek slyp hom
> totdat hy klink en blink.

Literally translated this stanza reads:

> I got a wee little chisel,
> I tapped it till it clinked;
> I sharpened it and sharpened it
> until it shone and clinked.

The poem continues to describe the vigour and vitality of the language, a language with which one can do so much. Then he ends with this vision:

> en op die dag sien ek die nag
> daar anderkant gaan oop
> met 'n bars wat van my beitel af
> dwarsdeur die sterre loop.

Literally translated, this means:

and on that day I saw the night
on the far side open up
with a crack running from my chisel
all through the stars.

Only when everybody who loves this language undertakes anew to use this valuable treasure fearlessly as a chisel, will we be able to cut out a future for ourselves with it. As the English poet Alexander Pope rightly said in his letter to Arbuthnot: "There is no language, except the language of the heart."

TWENTY

—*—*—*—*—

THE FLARE OF HOPE

The focal point of Christmas is and must always remain the Christ-child in his bed of straw, beckoning the world to return to the heart of God with his infant hand.

Christmas marks God's act of love, intended to heal and restore a world torn apart by sin. He who wants to remove Christ from Christmas will time and again tear a trapdoor of immeasurable personal loss into his life.

However, in the powerful Christmas drama there were lesser characters, fringe figures who nevertheless played important parts in the glorious events of Christmas. One of the most crucial was Mary, the young girl from Nazareth. Above all women she was blessed by God: a figure of suffering and a heroine of faith.

Throughout the life of this Child she lived between the extremes of deepest suffering and richest joy. In a way she represents women from all ages. Through sorrow and suffering she becomes the eternal bearer of Life. She groans in childbearing, but she conquers through her feminine nobility. She is always described as the weaker sex, but she is unconquerably strong in her love. It is always the woman who bears the flare of hope into the future!

N. P. van Wyk Louw rightly said in his radio play *Die dieper reg* (literally translated the title means "the deeper right"):

> Ek is die bloed wat deur die jare gaan,
> geslagte aan geslagte bind, die vrou.
> En in my kring van liefde, blydskap, hoop
> en baie pyn, bestaan 'n volk onsterflik.

Literally translated this stanza reads:

> I am the blood running through the years,
> binding generation to generation, woman.
> And in my circle of love, joy, hope
> and much pain, a nation exists immortally.

Mary was betrothed to Joseph and a virgin when an angel brought her the strange message that she would bear a child without Joseph having had any part in it.

We can only imagine how her thoughts must have tormented her before she revealed her pregnancy to the unsuspecting Joseph. What they said to each other is unknown, but we can imagine for ourselves what a traumatic experience it must have been for them.

Eventually Joseph accepted Mary's word. He

must have loved her very much. Tenderly he assisted her throughout that time, while the gossips whispered and grinned about Joseph's betrothed who was pregnant.

How it must have tortured the young couple and how could they ever have silenced the gossips? Who would have believed the story of the annunciation by an angel? It would only have made them appear even more ridiculous.

Then they went to Bethlehem for the census. Physically it must have been a via dolorosa for the pregnant Mary. However, at last the long journey was over and the search for lodgings in the overflowing Bethlehem began. Everybody had relatives or guests to house so that the young couple could not find lodgings anywhere. At last, by the charity of an innkeeper, they found a place in a stable. There in the stable the little Child was born on that first Christmas night.

Mary's cup of happiness overflowed: her well-formed little son lay cosily and warmly in her arms, his mouth at her full breast – and Joseph was also with her. Joseph with the callused hands of a carpenter and his awkward movements around the newborn baby – but Joseph with a heart overflowing with love and tenderness for his wife and the strange newborn Child.

Soon after this the young family had to flee to Egypt before the wrath of Herod: the mother with the newborn baby in the care of the faithful Joseph. At last God brought them back to Nazareth among the slanderers and gossips.

There was always something special about the Child Jesus: something divine and inexplicable. The Apocrypha, for example, tells how Jesus made two doves from clay while playing with his friends. He took them in his hand, blew over them and they flew away as living doves. How would Mary have explained such an event?

He was also a child who argued with the priests in the temple when he was a teenager. This gifted Child was obedient to his parents. Many a day Mary must have been very confused, but she kept on believing that she was a maidservant of the Lord and had a sacred calling.

In the life of Jesus there are sixteen lost years of which the Bible mentions nothing. Many scientists maintain that he studied with the Essenes on the coast of the Dead Sea and for that reason was called rabbi. Many a day Mary must have longed for her singular but gifted child.

When he started his earthly ministry at thirty his parents didn't see much of him. However, they regularly received news about the amazing things that he did: he healed the sick, made the blind see, the deaf hear and even awakened the dead! How would the simple country people have regarded the miracles of their Son?

Mary did see her Son again: when He was nailed to a rough wooden cross on Golgotha. Her mother's heart cringed with pain when the hammer-blows rang out and the crown of thorns was pressed onto his head. She must have wept at the raw mockery and abuses that he had to bear; she must have cried out when the cruel spear was pushed into his side. In the pain of his dying moments Jesus entrusted his mother to the care of the disciple John. It must have been a relief to her when at last he ended everything with the words: "It is finished."

And then she was flung to the other emotional extreme: what joy must have flowed over her when she saw him again after his triumphant resurrection and afterwards when he ascended to heaven in glory.

When we honour the Child of Bethlehem during Christmas, let us also honour the love and faithfulness of a mother as mirrored in one of the other characters in the Christmas scene: Mary, the virgin of Nazareth – the woman who bound the most meaningful words in language, "Jesus" and "mother" inextricably together.

TWENTY-ONE

—*—*—*—*—

TO LOOSEN THE SAILS

Thousands of mothers must annually live through a painful loosening process: the process of detaching themselves from matriculants who, for the last seventeen or so years, were bound to them by a symbiosis that can only exist between a mother and her child.

The reliance and commitment between mother and child is described thus by Elisabeth Eybers in her poem "Die moeder" (literally translated the title means "the mother"):

Die vreemde oorsprong van jou lewe het
soos lig deur 'n kristal deur my gevloei
in al die maande toe ek één was met
die stil geheim van jou verborge groei.

En nou kan niks ons skei – want is jy nie
afhanklik en gebonde aan my bloed
wat met sy onbegryplike chemié
jou wonderlik gevorm het en voed?

En of dié uur ver en vergete word,

en of die jare tussen jou en my
hul seile span, die see sy golwe stort,
of selfs die Dood sy somber baken steek,
nogtans sal jy aan my gebonde bly
met die onsigb're naelstring wat nie breek.

Literally translated this poem reads as follows:

The strange origin of your life flowed
like light through a crystal through me
in all the months when I was one with
the silent secret of your hidden growth.

And now nothing can separate us – for are you not
dependent and bound to my blood
that with its incredible chemistry
have formed and fed you miraculously?

And whether this hour becomes far and forgotten,
and whether the years between you and me
loosen their sails, and the sea hurls its breakers,
or even Death places its sombre beacon,
nevertheless you will remain bound to me
with the invisible cord that cannot break.

The moment of the "loosening of the sails" has arrived. In these days, it is quite understandable that the thoughts of mothers return to the birth of a child now in matric. May your children remain inseparably joined to you "with the invisible cord that cannot break."

It reminded me again of the birth of our last child, Lize. Shortly after Lize's birth I wrote a letter to my wife, Louise. This is the letter I wrote (a little baring of the soul hurts nobody):

"My Dearest, it is two o' clock in the morning and I cannot sleep because my thoughts keep on returning to you there in the maternity ward. I am so unspeakably proud of you and so thankful to the Good Giver.

"Thank you for the person you are and for the lovely children you have given me; for your tolerant love that has carried me through the years; a love that will also carry our children … and for the beautiful little girl you have now brought into our lives.

"It was wonderful last night to have come just in time and to have been able to help with the birth. I was so calm and full of inner peace. You were so brave, so beautiful and full of shining love.

"How will I ever be able to express my love for you … and how proud I was, how thankful towards you. Our cup is truly overflowing. It is as if suddenly a new dimension has come into our love, a dimension that no one can take away from us.

"It was a wonderful weekend. We stayed so near to each other; so united in these mystical, beautiful hours.

"Motherhood is without doubt one of the most beautiful things in God's creation – he surely meant it to be so. Now you must become strong and well before you come home, you and our dear Lize.

"Here at home the joy was exuberant. The children prattled about their mother with immeasurable pride. They were so excited that they sat with me until late at night to look up telephone numbers. They spread mattresses on the floor and came to sleep with Theo and me. We read the Bible together and they thought lovingly about their mother and sister. What an unforgettable moment.

"I hope you are resting well today. For me the day will be interminable at the Synod session. The children are wonderful: Solomon so adult, Nelda so possessive, Faffa so giggly and Theo such a big fellow. What would we have done without them – and now dear Lize is added!

"Thank You, Heavenly Giver! Look after yourself well, dear one. Be assured of my deepest and fondest love, a love so great that it hurts inside me because I cannot contain all of it.

"Yours as ever! S."

***

And before we knew it this helpless, innocent

bundle of love called Lize was grown up and her final year at school nearly completed.

The "sails were loosened."

New sensations overcome one. How is it possible that time could fly so quickly? This last year passed the swiftest of all: school-leavers' camp, interschool sports meetings, Rapportryers farewell dinner, "forty days," matric farewell, cramming time and then the exam.

Everything flashes through my mind: each exam; the days next to the rugby, netball or hockey fields of the primary school when you – despite being a rather reserved mother – cheered like a lunatic and ran up and down the field without inhibitions; the lines we played together, laughed together, cried together. You have always been there for our children.

Thus it will undoubtedly remain all through your life, because you are a mother. However, I think the farewell at this moment is one of the most painful.

I wish strength and courage for all the mothers who have to deal with the painful loosening of bonds that were formed so carefully over the years.

May the invisible cord that never breaks comfort you; may it be your strength and reward.

I know you can do it, because you have taught your children to be strong and handle crises successfully. Your anchors were so strong that they gave our children wings that will time and again carry them back to you lovingly and thankfully.

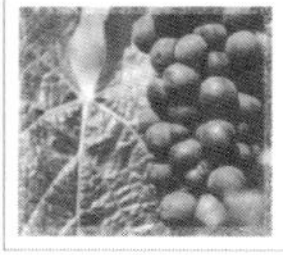

TWENTY-TWO

—*—*—*—*—

THE GRASS ON THE OTHER SIDE OF THE FENCE

In the aeroplane on the way to Windhoek I had the opportunity to read *The myth of the greener grass* by J. Allen Petersen again … and it awakened the same sense of dismay in me as it did the previous times.

The theme of the book is marital infidelity and it is a book especially for our time, because the waiting rooms of psychologists, doctors and ministers are filled with people bearing the scars that are the inevitable consequence of infidelity.

Nevertheless, society is increasingly accepting and condoning it as just a little adventure within marriage.

Petersen is an expert on this matter, because he has been adviser to families with extramarital relationship problems for more than forty years and has seen its destructive power at first hand.

Nowadays marital infidelity is the order of the day. However, condemning it is not a popular subject to speak or write about. You are immediately branded a spoilsport. However, the scars of this aberration are to be seen more clearly in our society than at any other time in history: on men and women and children. Instead of covering these wounds with shame, they are exposed shamelessly.

Petersen writes:

> A call to marital fidelity is like a lonely voice that calls to us in the sexual desert of our time. What was previously called adultery and carried a stigma of disgrace, is now only an "affair" – a nice sounding word which is whispered with amazement and excitement. Now it is "a relationship," no longer sin.

What was previously hidden – a secret that was well kept – is now being flaunted in headlines, is a popular theme on television programmes, a best-seller on bookshelves, as ordinary as a cold. Marriages are now "open"; divorces are "creative."

In television soap operas, in award-winning dramas and in novels somebody is forever jumping in or out of the bed of a third person.

To cheat and deceive in marriage is no longer a disgrace. It has been refined to an art and has a strangely romantic aura. Nowadays you must defend fidelity in marriage as if it is something abnormal. People who are faithful in marriage are spoken of in a mocking and derogatory way as if they are old-fashioned and behind the times.

The writer Charles R. Swindoll (*Come before winter)* told of a woman who went out for dinner together with seven other women. They were all enrolled for a course in French and their children were all at school.

One woman asked the others full of bravado, "Who of you has never been unfaithful to your husband during your entire married life?"

Only one put up her hand.

That evening one of the women told her husband about the incident. When she admitted that she wasn't the one who had put up her hand, he was very disappointed.

"But I have never been unfaithful to you," she assured him hastily.

"Why then didn't you put up your hand?" he wanted to know.

"I was too ashamed," was the answer.

Hereupon Swindoll remarks: "It is like being ashamed of good health while an epidemic is raging, or to come out of an earthquake unhurt and to be ashamed of it."

According to Robert J. Levin and Alexander Lowen, co-writers of an article in an American magazine, *Red book,* there are a number of ways in which infidelity wrecks the future of a family.

Infidelity causes endless pain and sorrow to your marriage partner. A true marriage is one in which a man and a woman are bound together inextricably by love – not by law. They accept responsibility for each other. They give themselves to each other for today and for tomorrow. They seek fulfilment only in each other.

The first breach in a marriage takes place when one partner seeks his or her intimacy and fulfilment – sexually and otherwise – somewhere else. The first big treachery is that the deed is kept secret. Time, money and physical energy are given to the secret lover. What is given there must of necessity be taken from the marriage.

The one who is betrayed pays in sorrow and pain for the pleasure of the betrayer. That is the lowest form of betrayal and the worst kind of pain that can be inflicted.

Infidelity tries to hide the real problem. It soothes the problems in a marriage without healing them. It treats the symptoms and not the problem. It camouflages the disease and simultaneously causes infection and aggravation. Troubled by the thought of a divorce or estrangement the betrayer feigns fidelity while he is seeking fulfilment outside marriage. This doesn't solve any problems but only causes many new ones.

Infidelity is destructive and humiliating to the self. Keeping up appearances and keeping the affair secret, insinuating that the marriage is being protected, is the worst form of deception that can be practised: self-deceit.

Deception always turns the person who is deceived into an opponent. A deceiver is always his own greatest enemy, because he breaks down his own personality and happiness into disaster. Deception is always a losing situation.

The danger is that lies become a way of life. Those who live like that are mortally ill and do not even feel feverish.

To seek intimacy outside of marriage is not at all right or allowable, even though it is glossed over.

Let us call it by its proper name: it is sin; it is adultery; it is a trampling of love. It doesn't simplify life, but complicates it.

Marital deception and self-deceit is not healthy – it is sick. It is not proof of independence and strength – it is proof of a deep-seated personality defect and a call for help.

It is not a game – it is adultery.

As Charles Swindoll said: "The grass on the other side of the fence may seem greener, but it is poison. A loving Father put the fence there with a good purpose!"